SUMMARY
of David D. Burns, M.D.'s
FEELING GOOD

The New Mood Therapy

by SUMOREADS

TABLE OF CONTENTS

Key Takeaway: Confront the illusion of absolute fairness to let go of your anger.

Key Takeaway: Question your self-defeating thoughts to overcome guilt.

Key Takeaway: There are no realistic depressions.

Key Takeaway: A self-defeating belief system predisposes you to relapse after recovery.

Key Takeaway: Examine your automatic thoughts to weed out your silent assumptions.

Key Takeaway: Ground your self-worth in your humanness to break a persistent need for approval.

Key Takeaway: Question the validity of your emotional dependency to nurture the more dependable self-love.

Key Takeaway: Discard your notion of worth to live more purposely.

Key Takeaway: Try being average to overcome perfectionism and find more satisfaction.

Key Takeaway: Confront the illogical thoughts that cause your sense of hopelessness to regain the will to live.

Key Takeaway: Rationalize your automatic thoughts and respond with empathy to reclaim the joy of everyday life.

EXECUTIVE SUMMARY

In his book *Feeling Good: The New Mood Therapy*, David D. Burns outlines the drug-free techniques anyone can use to elevate their mood, acquire a positive sense of well-being, and nurture an optimistic attitude toward life. Burns draws from the science of cognitive therapy to argue that all moods are created by thoughts, not circumstances, and that depression is a condition fashioned from pervasive negative thoughts.

Burns contends that nearly all negative feelings are outgrowths of thinking errors. He takes the reader through the ten most common cognitive distortions and explains how they affect feelings and behavior. He asserts that anyone can beat depression by confronting and restructuring the illogical and pessimistic thinking patterns at its root. He maintains that when depressive patients learn to counter their negative, automatic thoughts with thought-out rational responses, they usually experience an immediate lift in mood. With consistent practice, they can develop and sustain a positive outlook on life without taking any drugs.

This new edition of *Feeling Good* also contains an extensive guide to antidepressant drugs and mood stabilizers. Burns blames the current overreliance on antidepressant drugs on the mushrooming but unproven biological theory of depression. He argues that a combination of cognitive therapy and drugs works better than treatment approaches that rely on drugs alone.

INTRODUCTION

Key Takeaway: Cognitive therapy solves mental problems by targeting and restructuring unhealthy thought patterns.

Cognitive therapy is based on the premise that thoughts influence feelings, often more than circumstances. If you can change what you think about catastrophic loss, rejection, failure, or any other circumstance that seems beyond your control, you can change your mood, your productivity, and your attitude toward life.

Research studies indicate that cognitive therapy is at least as effective as drug-based treatments in reducing the symptoms of mood disorders such as depression. Cognitive therapy has also proved to be helpful in reducing the incidence of panic attacks and other anxiety disorders. Additionally, this psychological intervention has been shown to reduce the risk of relapse among patients treated with antidepressants.

PART I:
THEORY AND RESEARCH

Key Takeaway: Your thought patterns influence your mood.

Your cognition—what you think, believe, value, and the way you look at yourself and the world—creates your feelings. Optimistic thoughts—when you believe them—can give you a sudden lift in mood. You feel depressed when negativity dominates the way you see yourself and the world.

The negative thought patterns that create depression are often illogical and distanced from reality. If you can identify and eliminate the mental distortions creating your sense of inadequacy, you can begin to experience better moods.

Key Takeaway: Use the Burns Depression Checklist to diagnose your moods.

The Burns Depression Checklist is a quick and reliable way to a make a self-assessment of depression symptoms. It assesses the nature of your thoughts and feelings, the quality of your activities and relationships, the presence of depression symptoms that manifest as physical symptoms, and the dominance of suicidal urges. Any score under 10 is normal. A score above 75 indicates extreme depression.

Key Takeaway: Negative, irrational thoughts distort reality and cause depression.

The events and circumstances of your life can be positive, negative, or neutral. They do not have any meaning of their own. You give meaning to whatever happens in the way you process and understand it. How you interpret your world influences how you feel.

A realistic interpretation of negative events produces normal emotions such as sadness. An illogical interpretation of the same events causes an abnormal emotional reaction, part of which many be anxiety or depression. Depression is principally the outgrowth of thought patterns that do not conform to reality.

The ten cognitive distortions at the root of depression are:

1. All-or-nothing thinking: This is the tendency to see circumstances and personal qualities in absolutes. This disposition creates fear and feelings of inadequacy because things are rarely black or white.

2. Overgeneralization: When you overgeneralize, you view a negative event as part of a pattern that will keep recurring in the future.

3. Mental filter: When you filter out the positives in a situation and focus on the negative, it's easy to conclude the entire situation is negative and feel depressed.

4. Disqualifying the positive: Depressed patients often think up ways not just to negate, but to transform neutral and positive circumstances into negatives.

5. Jumping to conclusions: This is the tendency to make premature judgments that are not supported by facts—to read people's minds and imagine negative motives for their behavior or predict a negative future based on a few setbacks, for example.

6. Magnification and minimization: This is a thinking error that involves exaggerating fears and the consequences of mistakes and downplaying personal strengths. It creates feelings of inadequacy.

7. Emotional reasoning: When you are caught up in emotional reasoning, you use your emotions to validate your negative qualities or circumstances. The cognitive distortion here is obvious when you consider that thoughts create emotions.

8. Should statements: Thinking you must or should do something diminishes the very motivation you try to muster. It creates feelings of shame and guilt when you fall short of your expectations.

9. Labeling and mislabeling: This is the tendency to fit yourself in negative and simplistic categories based on your shortcomings. You create self-loathing when you label yourself and hostility when you label others.

10. Personalization: When you assume responsibility for circumstances you could not have created or controlled, you invite unnecessary feelings of guilt.

Negative thoughts that are both intensive and pervasive often precede a depressive state. A patient going through a depressive episode will be filled by feelings of inadequacy and will likely visualize a worthless past and a hopeless future. These feelings are often so powerful that they are easily confused for facts.

"Every time you feel depressed about something, try to identify a corresponding negative thought you had just prior to and during the depression. Because these thoughts have actually created your bad mood, by learning to restructure them, you can change your mood" (Kindle Locations 658-660).

PART II:
PRACTICAL APPLICATIONS

Key Takeaway: Combating depression starts with building self-esteem.

More than 80 percent of depressed patients view themselves as inadequate in their most important qualities—in their intelligence, looks, achievement, or strength. Because of their low self-esteem, they often magnify their mistakes and see them as evidence of their inadequacy. A depressed patient will feel like a failure when he flunks a test or defective when he encounters rejection.

Countering this sense of deficiency begins with the realization that achievements, attractiveness, or popularity do not earn you your self-worth. The corollary is that love and approval cannot negate your sense of worthlessness. The only way to build self-esteem is to counter your feelings of inadequacy by questioning the irrational thoughts behind them.

Key Takeaway: Evaluate your negative thoughts and answer back with rational responses to change the way you think about yourself.

You can get over your sense of inadequacy by confronting your mental distortions. Train yourself to listen to what you say about yourself and question the validity of your critical self-opinion.

The three-column technique is especially effective in helping people talk back to their irrational thoughts. On a three-column piece of paper, write the automatic negative thoughts that run through your head when things don't go according to your expectations—just the thought, not the accompanying emotion. Use the second column to identify the corresponding cognitive distortion in these thoughts—could be overgeneralization, all-or-nothing thinking, or negativity dominance.

Find a truthful and rational response to your thoughts and write it in the third column. If you thought you are a loser, for example, consider that you have performed well in the past, so this thought can't be true. If you can't find a rational response to an upsetting thought, postpone the exercise for later or ask a friend how they would respond.

Take this exercise every day to change the way you think, feel, and act. It is imperative to write down the thoughts, cognitive distortions, and rational responses to analyze them objectively. You can supplement this exercise with the use of a wrist counter to monitor how many times you get critical thoughts. Self-monitoring increases self-control and, over time, reduces the incidence of self-critical thoughts.

A good place to start to develop specific coping strategies is to stop labeling yourself. Labeling is a self-defeating strategy: it globalizes and personalizes your problems and distracts you from what you have to do to be better at what you criticize yourself for. The way to solve a problem is to define it, not to have it define you.

It helps to remember that no one is any one global quality. All human beings are constantly evolving, making mistakes, and improvising as they go.

Key Takeaway: Change what you think about your inaction to change the way you feel, the way you act.

Depression undermines the will to do anything. Unfortunately, when you procrastinate, you accomplish little, end up feeling worse about yourself, and do even less. Doing nothing sinks you further into a vicious cycle that can fuel depression for years.

The reason people procrastinate, the reason they sink deeper into motivational paralysis, lies in their thought patterns. If you think about why you feel unmotivated to tackle an accumulating pile of undone tasks, you'll identify a feeling of inadequacy, anxiety, or of being overwhelmed. And if you question these feelings, you will realize that they are fed by unreasonable thoughts about yourself and your reality.

When you challenge these thoughts and change your behavior in a way that positively influences what you think, you can change your mood and, consequently, gain the drive to do things. Attempting to do something—literally anything—helps adjust your defeatist attitude. It distracts you from your critical monologue and gives you the sense of control you need to do more.

Key Takeaway: Use a daily plan and procrastination sheet to beat your disposition to do nothing.

To overcome your tendency to do nothing, start by making a daily plan of simple activities for every hour of the day. At the end of the day, mark every completed activity with a rating for mastery or pleasure. Accomplishing just a portion of this daily schedule gives you a sense of satisfaction and self-reliance that elevates your mood and lessens your tendency to no nothing.

If you procrastinate because you think a task is difficult or unpleasant, an anti-procrastination sheet can challenge your negative predictions and get you moving. Take a sheet of paper and write down a percentage estimation of how difficult and unrewarding a task will be. Break down the task and complete the first step. When you are done, compare the actual level of difficulty you experienced and the pleasure you derived from the process to your prediction. When you realize that most of the things you have to do are less difficult and more satisfying than you predict, your motivation soars, as does your productivity.

Key Takeaway: Talk back to the irrational inner voice that causes your sense of worthlessness.

External criticism—no matter how specific or vicious cannot cause you any discomfort by itself. Criticism is either right or wrong. If it's right, it simply means that you have something to work on. If it's wrong, you only need to ignore it. Either way, there's no reason for it to upset you.

The negative thoughts you create in response to damaging comments are what put you down. The only reason these thoughts put you down is because they contain some form of mental error—be it overgeneralization, labeling, or any of the other mental distortions. If a supervisor's comments make you feel worthless, for example, chances are you exaggerated their importance, filtered out your other successes, or unrealistically predicted a bleak future based on the few remarks.

To overcome your fear of criticism, identify the negative thoughts you create when you receive critical remarks, tie them to the corresponding mental distortions, and counter their validity with rational responses.

The best way to cope with criticism is to take an investigative attitude. If you feel the criticism you face is vicious and unfounded, you can disarm your verbal attacker by asking them to be more specific in their opinion. Alternatively, you can find something in the criticism to agree with, even if it means agreeing in principle, and ask for more feedback. Responding defensively only escalates the verbal confrontation, and walking away often tugs at your self-esteem. When you ask for specifics or respond with empathy, you create an environment where negotiation with the critic is possible. If you're the one in the wrong, you get a chance to agree on a mutual solution.

Key Takeaway: Confront the illusion of absolute fairness to let go of your anger.

You don't have to internalize or outwardly express your anger. Either choice has detrimental effects on yourself or on your relationships with others. Instead, you can choose to control your feelings and not to create anger.

The source of your anger has nothing to do with what people do—no matter how infuriating their actions seem. The way you think about and interpret negative events is the source of your anger. If you *think* the person who cut you off in line is a jerk, you'll either retaliate or withdraw, the emotional response to which will be frustration or anger. If you analyze your thought pattern, you'll realize you labeled the person, overgeneralized his character, or passed a "shouldn't" judgment on him. These mental distortions are what create your anger.

People will often act—and events will often turn out—in ways you don't like. What is fair or unjust to you may seem right and necessary to the next person because fairness and justice are relative concepts. Absolute fairness and consistent reciprocity are impossible ideals. If you're angry, chances are you are confusing your preferences for a universally agreed-upon way of doing things. Before you make an emotional response to the hurtful actions of another person, ask yourself whether the actions are intentional and whether they are unnecessary from their point of view

The first step to coping with anger is to analyze the advantages and disadvantages of holding on to it. Consider if it is helping you achieve any objective or if it is just weighing you down and poisoning your relationships. When you understand the thoughts of the person infuriating you and the motivation of their actions, you can respond with empathy instead of anger.

The next is to weigh the thoughts creating your anger. Write the adversarial thoughts that create your anger and, for each thought, find and write an alternative and more rational thought. It helps to reconsider what you think is the fair treatment you are entitled to and to commit to take on a more realistic attitude. From this objective viewpoint, you can influence the behavior of the other person in an effective way—you can disarm them with agreements, clarify your point of view calmly, and issue ultimatums only as a last resort.

Key Takeaway: Question your self-defeating thoughts to overcome guilt.

Guilt is an abnormal deviation from the healthy feeling of remorse. If you feel guilty, you have taken it to mean that whatever action you committed or omitted violates your moral standards and somehow makes you a bad person. If you feel remorse, you understand that while whatever you did was hurtful, it does not reflect on your character. Guilt may escalate to depression when you interpret your bad behavior to mean you are worthless.

Guilt, like other negative emotions, feeds off mental distortions. Feelings of guilt may crop up when you magnify the badness of what you did, label yourself a bad person from a single incidence, or weigh the action with irrational "should" statements. Guilt may turn into a vicious cycle if you interpret your feelings of guilt to mean that you are a bad person and deserve to suffer for it.

Holding on to guilt is pointless because it does not make anything right by itself. You can choose to respond with empathy—with self-love and understanding—to what you consider inappropriate action. Consider if your action was intentional or if you are holding yourself to an irrational perfectionist ideal. If you are feeling guilty about upsetting someone, consider that you may be personalizing the incidence—their thoughts most likely upset them, not you. Record and confront other distorted thoughts causing your guilt. If you can fix the problem, make a plan to do so. If you can't, consider that you are bound to make mistakes by virtue of your humanness.

PART III:
"REALISTIC" DEPRESSIONS

Key Takeaway: There are no realistic depressions.

No negative event—be it the death of a loved one, terminal illness, or bankruptcy—is bad enough to cause "realistic" depression. When interpreted realistically, events that involve loss or disappointment can only create sadness, which is a normal, time-bound emotion. Interpreted in any distorted way—if the victim takes the undesirable event to mean he or she will never be happy again, for example— these events create feelings of hopelessness and lead to depression, which can persist indefinitely.

When people are incapacitated by severe illness, it is not the illness itself that causes their despondency. It is the thought that they are not making any contributions where they *should* that creates frustration, anger, and guilt. These thought patterns are illogical because they tie the person's self-worth to her work and contributions. If human worth were something people had to work for, what would be the value of infants? Personal worth is constant through illness and strife. It is only challenged by distorted thoughts.

It may seem realistic to feel empty after an amputation or loss of a loved one. But this feeling grows from the irrational thought that you will experience less joy after your loss. The thought is unrealistic because it filters out all other sources of joy in your life. To think you will be joyless is to discount the positives in your life, to jump to premature conclusions, and to exaggerate the magnitude of your loss. When you question these thoughts and focus on the things you can still do and find joy in, you lessen your gloom.

PART IV:
PREVENTION AND PERSONAL GROWTH

Key Takeaway: A self-defeating belief system predisposes you to relapse after recovery.

You *feel* better when you challenge your distorted thoughts and vanquish your mood swings. You *get* better when you understand why you got depressed in the first place and continually reapply the techniques that led to your transformation.

The silent assumptions that make up your mental model may cause you to relapse if left unaddressed. If you tie your self-esteem to your achievements, to perfectionism, or to the love and approval you get from others, for example, you expose yourself to a depressive state every time one of these ideals is threatened.

Getting better takes a commitment to address the deeper assumptions that caused your depression and to work toward reacquiring your self-confidence and self-esteem.

Key Takeaway: Examine your automatic thoughts to weed out your silent assumptions.

To find out what your mental model is built on, identify the automatic thoughts causing your anger, anxiety, or any other undesirable emotional response. Instead of countering this thought with a rational response, ask yourself why that thought would upset you, assuming it were true. Ask yourself what this new thought would mean and keep going until you get to the core beliefs that feed your thoughts.

Key Takeaway: Ground your self-worth in your humanness to break a persistent need for approval.

What other people say about you only affects your mood if you believe it to be true. If you feel threatened by someone's disapproval, it is only because you take it to mean something really is wrong with you and that everyone else will ultimately reject you.

If you believe approval ties to your worth, you will be elevated by every positive remark and crushed by every disapproving comment. This emotional rollercoaster easily leads to depression.

Most of the time, people disapprove of you only because they made an irrational assessment of your character. Even if they are right in their assessment, they are only right about a specific part of you, not your worth as a person.

A cost-benefit analysis of your beliefs can help challenge your need for approval. List all the ways the belief that you should act in ways people approve of serves and doesn't serve you. When you recognize all the ways this belief limits you, frame approval as something that would be nice to have but that doesn't tie to your worth.

You can also use a wrist counter to monitor all the good things you notice about yourself without external validation. Over time, self-monitoring builds your self-approval.

Key Takeaway: Question the validity of your emotional dependency to nurture the more dependable self-love.

When you tie your happiness and worth to the love you get from others, you give up both the responsibility and the security of your emotional life. Since no one can be consistently affectionate towards you all the time, you expose your self-esteem to needless blows.

To take back control of your emotional life, identify the reasons for your love dependency and counter them with rational reasons for why this need may incapacitate you. It helps to recognize that self-love is a more dependable form of love, that only you can make yourself sustainably happy, and that being alone does not mean you are lonely.

It also helps to remember that most of life's pleasures are enjoyable whether you experience them alone or with someone. When you cultivate self-love—by treating yourself like you would someone you love and committing to enjoy life by yourself—you radiate a joy that attracts other people to you.

"The more independent you are, the more secure you will be in your feelings. Furthermore, your moods will not go up and down at someone else's mercy" (Kindle Locations 4733-4734).

Key Takeaway: Discard your notion of worth to live more purposely.

The silent assumption that your personal worth ties to your accomplishments is both inaccurate and emotionally injurious. Personal worth and achievement are unrelated subjective concepts. The assumption that people who achieve more are somehow better only creates a work addiction that undermines quality of life.

A cost-benefit analysis of this belief can help you discard it. Tying your achievements to your worth could motivate you to be more productive—and it certainly would make you feel better about yourself when you won. But it also means you would focus on your work at the expense of other sources of satisfaction, such as family. It also means you would feel worthless when you don't live up to your desired level of achievement. You would constantly need more achievement to feel settled—a pursuit that would turn your life into a race with an impossible end.

Personal worth is a subjective abstraction that remains constant through life's cycles. You can't add to your self-worth, and you can only take from it if you barrage it with irrational thoughts. It is infinitely more gratifying to pursue the adventure, joy, learning, and personal growth of everyday life than to pursue an elusive sense of worth.

Key Takeaway: Try being average to overcome perfectionism and find more satisfaction.

Perfectionism is an illusion, a trap hallway that only leads to disappointment. If you tie your worth to how well you do things, the only thing you are guaranteed is countless blows to your self-esteem when what you do falls below your standards.

To overcome perfectionism, make a comparative list with the advantages and disadvantages of chasing it. This comparison can show you why the illusion doesn't serve you. You will discover that striving for perfection doesn't help you get more done or give you more satisfaction. When you get the urge to do something perfectly, try sitting with the discomfort of doing nothing. In time, the compulsion subsides and disappears.

When you pursue averageness instead of perfectionism, you take on an easier attitude and find more joy in your work. It will surprise you to find that you do better and produce more when you lower your standards.

Part of overcoming perfectionism is evaluating your work based on what you can control—which is the process, not the outcome—and setting realistic process goals.

It's the unrealistic expectations you set—not your shortcomings—that upset you. If you assess some of your most enjoyable moments, you will discover that they were full of imperfections.

PART V:
DEFEATING HOPELESSNESS AND SUICIDE

Key Takeaway: Confront the illogical thoughts that cause your sense of hopelessness to regain the will to live.

Depression distorts memories of the past and fills images of the future with pervasive hopelessness. The gloom of the present often convinces depressed patients that their "real" selves have never been happy a day of their lives. Suicidal urges grow out of the ensuing illogical conviction that their moods will never get better.

Individuals at a high risk of suicide are those who feel severely depressed, those who actively plan to commit suicide or have attempted suicide in the past, and those who feel there's nothing to deter them from committing suicide. It's imperative that anyone in any of these categories seek immediate professional help.

If you are willing to explore the problem you think is unsolvable, you can find the illogical thoughts that trigger your sense of hopelessness, restructure them into realistic thoughts, and reacquire the will to live.

Depressive patients who contemplate suicide often mistake the symptoms of their hopelessness—such as apathy and feelings of worthlessness—for evidence of their real identity and worth. They magnify the effect of their condition, disqualify their accomplishments, rush to predict a bleak future, and entertain a host of other mental distortions. These illogical thoughts feed the conviction that there's no point in living. When patients commit to correct these cognitive errors, their mood swings usually subside.

PART VI:
COPING WITH THE STRESSES AND STRAINS OF DAILY LIVING

Key Takeaway: Rationalize your automatic thoughts and respond with empathy to reclaim the joy of everyday life.

Unwanted emotions can pile up and drain you. This is especially if you work in an emotionally tense environment such as that of a psychiatrist or an air-traffic controller. The two-column technique can help you get a handle on undesirable emotions. Write your automatic negative thoughts on one column then think up rational responses to these thoughts and write them in the second column.

You can learn to cope with difficult people by practicing the disarming technique. Urge them to let out their negative feelings then find some truth in their anger or criticism and agree with it. Point out what you disagree with in a non-argumentative way, and then assert that you can still get along despite the disagreements. It helps to try to see the other person's point of view and motivations. Often, you will realize that angry outbursts and unwarranted criticisms are projections of their fears or frustrations and have little to do with you.

PART VII:
THE CHEMISTRY OF MOOD

Key Takeaway: The chemical imbalance perception of depression is an unproven theory.

While researchers have established that genetic factors have a significant influence on the occurrence of manic-depressive illness, evidence for the influence of genetic factors on common forms of depression is scanty.

The exact causes of depression remain elusive because scientists are yet to understand how the human brain really works. One of the main theories that attempts to explain depression proposes that the illness is caused by a deficiency of one of the biogenic amine transmitter substances in the brain. These substances—serotonin, dopamine, and norepinephrine—act as chemical messengers in the part of the brain that processes emotions.

Scientists think that antidepressant drugs elevate mood by boosting the levels of these chemical messengers. Other scientists maintain that these drugs work by stimulating nerves—the "wires" that transmit electrical signals in the brain. It's difficult to understand exactly how these drugs work because they interact with the chemicals in the brain in thousands of ways.

Key Takeaway: Treatment that combines antidepressants and psychotherapy works better than a strict drug approach.

Cognitive therapy and drug treatment work well to lessen depressive symptoms during the period of treatment. After recovery, patients who went for cognitive therapy or combined it with antidepressants are likely to forestall depressive symptoms for longer than those who only took antidepressants. Psychotherapy, it would seem, equips patients with coping skills and prepares them to handle everyday strains long after recovery.

For some types of depression, drugs complement psychotherapy and make it easier for patients to identify and question their irrational thoughts.

"The combination of drugs and psychotherapy can work better and quicker than drugs alone and frequently leads to better long-term results. This seems to be true for mildly depressed patients and for severely depressed patients as well" (Kindle Locations 6943-6944).

Key Takeaway: Unfounded myths usually interfere with depression treatment.

The myths that demonize either form of treatment are largely untrue. Most antidepressants are safe and stable—the side effects are barely noticeable, patients don't experience adverse reactions or abnormal mood changes, and the risk of developing an addiction is nonexistent.

There's nothing shameful about taking antidepressants or going for psychotherapy. Depression is a serious illness that can adversely affect multiple areas of your life if left unaddressed. Treatment works even for "real" problems that seem hopeless.

Key Takeaway: Monitor your recovery progress to know what treatment works for you.

If given the right prescription and dosage, any patient can expect to respond positively to antidepressant drugs. Approximately 60 to 70 percent of patients experience improvements in mood after taking these drugs for a minimum of two or three weeks. Taking a depression test periodically—once or twice a week—can tell you if you are responding well to treatment.

If there's no substantial improvement in mood in four or five weeks, you could be on the wrong dosage or medication. Checking the blood level of the antidepressant regularly can tell you if you are on an effective dosage. Differences in genetics, weather, age, body weight, kidney function, and other metabolic processes influence the blood levels of drugs.

If the dosage is right but you are still not responding, your doctor may consider augmenting your treatment with small doses of a different drug or switching you to another class of antidepressants. Treatment is considered successful if your score on the depression test falls to the normal or happy range. When treatment is successful, your doctor should make a plan to reduce your dosage (to avoid uncomfortable withdrawal reactions) and eventually get you off antidepressants.

Caution should be exercised when taking antidepressants or mood stabilizers alongside other drugs. These drugs may interact and lower effectiveness of the antidepressants or cause dangerous side effects.

Key Takeaway: The cost of antidepressants does not reflect their effectiveness.

The most expensive antidepressants are not necessarily the most effective. Newer drugs are relatively more expensive than older ones because their patents—which give exclusive production rights to one company—are still valid. Despite vast cost differences, most antidepressants are comparably effective. The key benefit of newer, more expensive drugs is in that they may have fewer side effects.

The cost of the same generic drugs also varies depending on the manufacturer. If you can get a prescription of the drugs you need in their chemical rather than brand names, your druggist may get you the inexpensive option.

EDITORIAL REVIEW

As early as the first century, the Greek philosopher Epictetus had postulated that people are distressed not by their circumstances but by the way they think about them. In the 1950s, Albert Ellis advanced the burgeoning philosophical approach to psychotherapy when he proposed a model built on the premise that irrational, self-defeating beliefs are the source of emotional pain.

Years later, Dr. Aaron T. Beck—renowned psychiatrist and David D. Burns' mentor—realized that his patients were depressed because they hardly reflected on or challenged negative thoughts about themselves, the world, and their future. Beck furthered research into automatic, negative thoughts and found that depressed patients could feel better and act more functionally if they were taught to think more realistically about their circumstances. His research sparked off the cognitive therapy movement.

David D. Burns builds on Aaron T. Beck's ideas to demystify cognitive therapy and make its techniques accessible to the masses and more palatable to critics. In *Feeling Good: The New Mood Therapy*, he argues that cognitive therapy is at least as (if not more) effective in treating mood disorders as drug-based approaches. He challenges the biochemical theories of depression and maintains that patients can alleviate their depressive symptoms by learning to confront and rebut their negative thoughts.

Burns argues that virtually every negative feeling can be tied to a thinking error. He explains ten of the most common cognitive distortions and encourages readers to refer back to them whenever they are feeling anxious, angry, defeated, or worthless. He uses role-play dialogues to illustrate the absurdity of irrational thought patterns (such as overgeneralization, labeling, and mental filters) and to explain how to put a concept or skill to work. He accompanies these dialogues with real patient cases to show how individuals can confront their mental distortions and abate their depressive symptoms.

Feeling Good also includes a comprehensive review of the costs, recommended doses, and side effects of common antidepressants and mood stabilizing drugs. This review is meant to serve as a guide for readers who wish to combine cognitive therapy with medications.

Feeling Good comes in the wake of a growing pile of research on the effectiveness of bibliotherapy—the use of books as a form of psychotherapy. Some of these studies, which Burns cites in his work, have demonstrated that reading a book on depression may be as useful as consulting a therapist. In fact, depressive patients who read *Feeling Good* over a period of four weeks reported a 20 percent improvement in their symptoms.

Burns set out to write a comprehensive guide to depression. In the end, he does more than that. *Feeling Good* is a practical guide to everyday emotional turmoil—whether that turmoil is caused by loss, disappointment, or by the hostility of difficult people.

ABOUT THE AUTHOR

David D. Burns is a clinical psychiatrist and author of the best-selling books *Feeling Good* and *The Feeling Good Handbook* and eight other bibliotherapy titles. He is an adjunct professor emeritus at Stanford University School of Medicine where he is involved in behavioral sciences research and training.

THE END

If you enjoyed this summary, please leave an honest review on Amazon.com…it'd mean a lot to us.

If you haven't already, we encourage you to purchase a copy of the original book.

Made in the USA
Lexington, KY
01 March 2019